Top Jobs For Stay-At-Home-Moms

The information you needed and then some more...

Table of Contents

INTRODUCTION: WHY SHOULD YOU READ THIS EBOOK?

You are reading this eBook because you want to find ways to make money while you take care of your children at home. Though this book is titled, "Top Jobs For Stay-at-Home Moms", it is actually an excellent resource for ALL parents who want to stay at home and work while watching their children grow.

Single moms have it tough. They are young, often have no other fall-back system and are constantly fighting to pay for their children's expenses, which will not wait nor adjust to the pocket size. The Internet is full of "legitimate jobs", but as you will learn quickly enough, the majority are scams. Unless you are careful, you will end up spending more than you earn chasing dreams and false promises.

This book is designed for those who need help with ideas, real time resources and jobs that pay the bills. Most single parents are not afraid to work hard, but they do not know where to start and which site to trust. You will find here tried-and-tested ideas on how to start earning from home as well as information about jobs you could take up while staying at home looking after your babies.

The information compiled here will set you free financially. It will also tell you what you need to do to ensure you earn while working at home. Your income will still depend upon the type of work you choose and the hours you can put in, but with the help of this book, you will be able to maximize the returns on your effort.

Hope you enjoy reading this book as much as I enjoyed putting it together. Happy reading!

CHAPTER 1: WORKING FROM HOME 101

Most people think working from home is child's play. In other words, if you are working from home, the "work" is actually easy. The very first thing you need to do when you have decided that working-from-home is the only (or the best) thing for you is to learn what it takes.

5 Myths Exploded

There are many myths about working-at-home; to be successful and optimize your income, you need to be separate the myth from the truth. Life is harsh when you are faced with financial challenges and any misconception about working-at-home jobs and businesses can develop into extremely stressful situations.

Myth 1: I will have all the time in the world to do my work.

The Truth: Wrong! Staying at home means you are hands-on 24x7. Your babies will demand your attention constantly and you will actually wonder how other moms cope with their children when you need 48 hours' work crammed into your 24 hours day. To ensure you get any financially-productive work done, you need to set hard rules about work time or no interruption time. You will need to make the effort to make time.

Myth 2: Being my own boss means I can it easy.

The Truth: Being your own boss is even more demanding than working for one. You will soon realize that no work means no money. Also, that often time means money, more time means more money. Suddenly it will dawn on you that being your own boss means you have to generate your funds;

there is no one to pass on the buck to – only you. This is some heavy-duty responsibility.

Myth 3: I can earn big money with at-home jobs, for doing half the work demanded in a regular job.

The Truth: While it is 100% true that work-at-home-jobs provide a platform where you can earn many times over what you would be making in a regular job, it is NOT true that you would be working half the time. The beauty of working at home is that you can work many more hours and earn much more.

To earn more is possible; but to do so, you would have to work twice as hard. You cannot afford any slack because the moment you relax you lose money. Working at home means you have to be more responsible, more organized and definitely more hardworking.

Myth 4: I will work when my children go to sleep.

The Truth: have you heard about the saying, "A watched pot never boils"? Well, that is exactly what is going to happen. Everyone else's children will sleep peacefully at noon or at night; yours won't. You need to weave a flexible schedule where you have no certainties about time. Not only the children would not sleep at the right time, but also sometimes, you would have emergencies, which will further throw your schedule off the track.

Working from home means being innovative about how you use your time.

Myth 5: Work-at-home means I do not have to worry about bookkeeping and accounts.

The Truth: You will have to be more careful than ever. Your income may not resemble – at least initially – the paycheck of a regular job hence it is easy to become complacent. Don't! You will have massive problems with filing your taxes unless you are careful to note every expense incurred for setting up your home office, as well as income received for your services and/ or products. Use a professional software or person to get you on the right track.

The Dos And Don'ts Of Working At Home

If and when you choose to work from home, you need to lay down some ground rules. These rules will help you work better and involve the help and cooperation of your family and friends.

The Do's Of Working At Home

DO Draw Up A Road Map – working at home requires that you plan your time very carefully to ensure that you achieve what you set out to do, complete the task you have undertaken and are able to generate a comfortable income. Let us say, you need about $5,000 per month and you want to work 5 days a week.

This means you would have to work out something that gives you $250 per day on an average. Now, you will have to find out ways that will earn you this amount. You will find that it is much easier to work when you have a well-defined goal in front of you.

DO Find Out The Best Time You Can Work – as a mom, you would have plenty of chores to do, which cannot be set aside to accommodate work. Things like cooking, cleaning the house, helping with homework, homeschooling, ensuring that children sleep in time, and so on will have you on your feet for the best part of the day. You need to find a window in your daily routine, when you could focus on your work without interruption or worry.

Most moms find night time the best for work. In that case, you ensure you have enough sleep as sleep deprivation has very serious health consequences.

DO Have A Place Dedicated To Work – you may not need a specific office, though it would be good if you can reserve a room for this purpose. You do need to have a corner in your home reserved as your work space. Organize this space to include whatever you need for your work so you would not waste time searching for things, tools or documents when you work.

DO Make It Clear That Work Time If Off For Children – this might not be possible if you have very young children. However, if they are old enough, they should know that the time you work is when you should not disturbed unless for emergencies.

DO Ensure That The Children Are Safe When You Are Working – it is very important that you ensure that the children are safe when you are off to work. If the children are very young, it is best to set up you work place close to the nursery so you could keep an eye on them at all time. For younger children, best time is after they sleep at night, when they go to school or take their afternoon nap.

You could work out with neighbors/ friends/ family with babies to exchange babysitting time so everyone can get their work done. With a little coordination this could become an exceptionally good arrangement.

DO Set Up A Saving Fund For Rainy Days – you need to save enough funds to support you and your family for about 6-12 months in case all income stops. I know it sounds utopian when you're struggling to earn a decent income from home, but it is very important that you have something put aside not only for down days, but also for emergencies such as accidents, illness, etc.

The Don'ts Of Working At Home

DON'T Work Sporadically Or As Per Mood – believe me, unless you set time aside you will never get enough time to work. You will always have something to finish or you would feel too tired, too depressed, too harried to get to work and the work would never get done.

DON'T Mix Business With Pleasure – you cannot do two important tasks at the same time and do a good job with both. No matter how much you try, one or other task will fall short of your expectations. When you look after the children and home, do not work and vice versa. If you don't separate the two you will end up frustrated with both.

DON'T Lose Heart When Things Go Slow – there will be times when things do not go the way you plan, when money will be less than expected, when bills will overwhelm you. Don't lose heart. Ups and downs are part of life and with a little perseverance you'll come out a winner.

CHAPTER 2: OPTIONS FOR STAY-AT-HOME MOMS

You would have noticed that the title does not stay-at-home *"jobs"*; it says, *"productive occupation"*. This is because while you would be to find a huge number of online jobs, which you could take from home, the best option would always be to launch you own home-based business.

A survey carried out in 2001 by *The Entrepreneurial Parent*, interviewed about 600 respondents from all over the country. The findings were very encouraging; 1 out of 7 respondents stated that they were making close to $100,000 annually working about 40 hours per week. A more recent study showed that small home businesses generate on an average $63,000 annual income.

Micro-Business Ideas

Micro business ideas are called thus because they are at the tiniest level. This is what every mom can start almost right away. Every person in this world is good at something. Some people might know right away, say a hobby or something that gives them immense pleasure. Some may have to discover it.

Make a list of top 10 things you would like to do, if you did not have to work for money. Look closely at the list. Choose 5 that you think would be in demand if sold and then prioritize them in order of your preference. Focus on the first one or two. Let us say, you love knitting, cooking, tutoring, writing, travelling, event management, photography, etc. Choose the one you like most and that's your idea for micro business.

Much too often I hear that young moms feel they don't have anything much to show as a special talent. It's not true. Everyone is unique and has some talent. You do, too. You need to believe in yourself and get out there and become an expert at that one thing. The reason why this is a great idea is because you'll love working for this and hence, you can work more while enjoying every moment of it.

Do not worry about its saleability; everything is saleable, especially on the Net. Once, you made up your mind about it, you get it online. We will talk about this subsequently. The important thing is to believe you can and apply yourself 100% percent to bring it to fruition. Let us look at a few common hobbies and how you could earn from doing what you love:

- **Cooking** - you can start sharing recipes online, provide online orders with homemade special snacks or meals, could take care of the food for parties, make handmade chocolate or food hampers for gifts, and so on.

- **Shopping** – you could start a review site for the local shops initially stating what is good and what is not, when there are sales, discounts and where there are great offers available. You could become a fashion consultant, mystery shopper, etc.

- **Fishing** – you could start a fishing trip management site where you could organize the most amazing fishing trips for groups of men, families, single men, etc. You could also have a blog on fishing with advice for fishing, place to fish and benefits of a fishing vacation with reviews and descriptions of the best fishing locations in and around your place of residence.

These are just a few examples off my head. There are plenty more in your mind. Choose one, or you can even choose two and focus on these hobbies to make money. You will find that you are not only having a lot of fun, but also earning enough to take care of your family.

Get Your Hobby Online

Whatever you like to do, there would be someone interested. People need to learn about it and for people to do so, they need your business online.

For a step-by-step free guide, check here - https://www.udemy.com/courses/search/?q=free+courses+on+how+start+a+business&p=2&sort=popularity&price=price-free&view=grid.

Launch An eBay Shop

eBay is a tried and tested place to sell anything you have. You can make craft, sell things you do not require around your home, things you buy wholesale and so on. The greatest thing about eBay is that it will charge you a nominal fee after you sell your wares.

Another plus point here is that eBay provides a huge number of tutorials, free of cost, for all those who want to learn to sell on eBay. Their back-office support is excellent and you can learn and earn pretty quickly.

Like eBay there are now 1001 online shops, which do as good a job if not better than eBay. Do not get stuck with eBay only; shop around, you might find better.

Online Consultant

Are you an expert at anything? One smart stay-at-home mom hit the jackpot by giving consultation on how to put babies to sleep. This is a thing that many moms would think mommies knew. Guess what? Many moms would give a hand and a leg to learn how to effectively put the baby to sleep. Nothing is too trivial. If you know something, someone, somewhere in the world would want to know about it. That's the beauty of the Net – it gives you the world as your market.

Online Travel Agency

Travelling is perhaps one of the most sought after leisure activity in the world. It is also important for industries, corporate houses and business men. No wonder this is one of the most lucrative online businesses the world over. The good news is that anyone can start this business with a minimal investment.

Check out http://www.ptstravel.com/ to have an idea. I am not endorsing this option, not have I tried it, but it will give you an idea of what it takes to start an online travel agency.

With the travel agency you could start a place/ hotel/ restaurant rating blog where your clients could share their experiences and rate the places they visited and you can earn a fortune through your blog as well.

Jobs That Will Always Be There

Online Tutoring

Tutoring is something that will not go out of fashion too soon. Education is as important as ever and students (and their parents) are always on the lookout for a better way to learn the subject matter. Are you an expert on any subject? You can start an online tutorial anytime you want. Check out the following sites for this purpose – Google Helpouts, Lynda, SkillShare, InstaEdu, TutorVista, Tutor and Udemy. For guidance on how should you start an online tutorial business, check this out - http://www.dltoben.com/tutorials/2908669-udemy-how-to-start-a-tutoring-business-easy-self-employed-income-2015.html.

Pet Care/ Pet Shelter With Selling Option

Are you an animal lover? You can turn this into a business, which will give you both satisfaction and money. Start an animal shelter and rescue animals from abuse, train them and sell them to people who appreciate them.

You can also provide accommodation for people who need pet sitting while they go on vacation or business trips. For a fee you could provide the beloved pets a warm and friendly environment while their owners are away.

You could also provide neutering/ spaying services, pet grooming services,

Photography Services

This is another fun-filled way to earn money that has remained in demand for as long as you can remember. Everyone wants to have memories of any special event in their lives. If you price your services reasonably and deliver good quality, your neighborhood itself should provide you with more business than you could handle.

Whether it is a baby shower, bachelor party, marriage, birthday or a funeral make sure your neighborhood know about your talent and business. With a regular camera, an online (free) photography course, excellent editing software and a good portfolio, you would be in business in no time.

Build a niche and become an expert in your area if you want to stay on the top of your competition.

Childcare

Childcare will always be in high demand. Just as you are in need of help with the children, all moms will at some time or other need help with babysitting. You could launch a website listing babysitters and nanny's available on call. It is important to verify the background of the people you recommend and work along with the local police while registering each person, lest there would be any mishaps inadvertently.

Senior Care

Some people would prefer that their parents live with them in their senior years. However, they find themselves in a quandary as the senior loved one cannot be left alone at home lest he or she would be harmed somehow; neither can they take leave to stay with the senior person. A nurse/ companion/ domestic help hired for this purpose can do the needful.

You may get trained (and licensed if necessary) and skilled yourself, or you could enroll people who are interested in such jobs for a fee and provide the services for a fee.

Home Made Beauty Aid Products

With the gradual and steady shift to all-natural ingredient products, handmade, customized, high quality beauty aid products are in high demand. You could take up an online course or download a few free eBooks on how-to make soaps, body scrubs, hair tonic, deodorants, lip balm, etc. and sell them to a good profit on the net.

Beauty hampers go well with green household cleaning products, which is another area you could explore.

Debt Collection Agency

This is another business than anyone can start right from scratch. All you need here is a phone, a computer and Internet. Payment is commensurate to the amount recovered and you will learn in time how to manage to get the money out, while still being as empathic as possible.

It's relatively easy; you need to be firm yet kind and follow the rules laid down by the Far Debt Collection Practices Act, which you should know well.

Franchise Business

The Franchise business is one of the hot favorites because of two things:

(i) it is easy to set up because you receive the model of the business, training, and all support you need to replicate the original;

(ii) it already has an established name, so you need worry about marketing it too much.

The downside is that it might require some investment. Look around for something you can do, love to do and if you the money to invest, there is little risk in taking up a franchisee. For some quick examples, check out a few examples given in the "Helpful Resources" at the end of the book.

Thinking Out-Of-The Box

Some of the best ideas for stay at home moms were innovations meant to provide solutions to local or personal problems. Look around in your neighborhood. Look at some of the problems you are facing right now and make a list. Can you provide solutions to any of these? If yes, you have a business idea.

For example, menu planner for parties, income tax consultant, party card invitations, handmade gifts, event manager for birthdays, baby photography, pet photography, etc. The list is endless. Use your talents to provide solutions to present and local problems. You cannot miss.

It may take a little time to find the right one for you, but you can do it. Brainstorm with some of your friends, conduct a few small surveys to see what the moms (and people in general) want help with. What are the problems they face where solutions could be offered/ worked out?

CHAPTER 3: TOP JOBS FOR STAY-AT-HOME MOMS

5 Red Flags That Will Identify A Scam

When you type is "jobs for stay-at-home moms" you will be flooded with results, each promising the best and most lucrative options. Be aware that more 80 percent of the advertised sites are scams. The mere 20 percent is often lost in the deluge of fraud offers. Before you sign up for any work, keep in mind the following red flags that could save you from heartache and loss of your hard earned money.

Asks You A Fee To Access The Job Board

There are job boards that promise you best match for your talents, but to get in you need to pay an upfront fee. Red flag! While it is possible that the job board might be genuine, it is more likely that it is not. Most genuine job boards allow access for free and provide special services for members for a fee.

Promises You Too Much For Too Less

If they promise too high a pay for too less work, it is more likely a scam than a great find. There are no free lunches in this world and get-rich-quick schemes are successful because too many people have too romantic ideas about life. Be very careful when you are offered opportunities to earn in 5-figures doing next-to-nothing; especially if you have to pay to become a member of the scheme.

Asks You Work For Free – Initially

If the site asks you to work for free, it should raise a red flag. Genuine sites pay for the work they require, even if it is for test purposes. This is most common for writers, copywriters, web designers, etc. who may be coaxed into doing something as a "test" before they are hired.

If the pay offered is very attractive, I have seen even veterans falling for this trick. When prospective clients ask for anything free, it is best to provide samples of past work. This should be enough for anyone to gather an idea about your ability to deliver. If they still insist that you do a certain assignment for free, it is a scam.

There Is No Upfront Payment

In most cases, an advance is warranted. You could ask for anything between 10% and 25% as booking advance. This would ensure that the client does not change his mind or deny payment later. Alternatively, you could break the assignment in small parts that would require payment on delivery.

There Are Too Many Clauses To Fulfill

Always take time to read the fine print. If you find that there are too many clauses that need to be fulfilled, ask the clients to change them. Do not fall for the "it's only a legal formality". You might get trapped into one such clauses and be cheated out of your hard earned money.

Job Boards For You

Of course, many people still love jobs. Since you cannot attend a 9 to 5 regular job, the best for you would be a remote one. Jobs are excellent for one reason – it ensures that at the end of the month there is a paycheck. Sometimes, just knowing that you have a paycheck coming will give you enough strength to do better and more. For those who prefer jobs to any other method to earn, check the following job boards.

It is especially useful to find out as many genuine and regularly updated job boards if you want to land a great job.

Remote Work Job Boards

DreamHomeBased **Work** (http://www.dreamhomebasedwork.com/work-at-home-job-leads.html) - you will find here all types of work that you can take up as a stay-at-home mom. The job are organized well, updated regularly and you have some very interesting articles to guide you as well.

FlexJobs (http://www.flexjobs.com/) - with more than 50 categories of jobs this site lists part-time, entry-level, middle-level and executive jobs. The great thing about this site is that they screen every listing to ensure that they are genuine. With more than 20,000 listings, this is a great place to look for opportunities.

Remote (https://weworkremotely.com/) – this list has it all from web design, to customer service to heavy-duty programming. Check the telltale subtag, "Office Not Required".

Skip The Drive (http://www.skipthedrive.com/) – this is a decent job board with opportunities that will help the newbie and the experienced alike to find jobs.

Staff.com (https://www.staff.com/) – the site has a service that matches your cv with the recruiters to make your task to find a job easier. It mostly offers long-term jobs in a wide range of industries. You may choose to work 80 hours part-time or 160 ours full time.

Virtual Vocations (http://www.virtualvocations.com/) – this site is started and run by a stay-at-home mom who felt frustrated about not finding a good site to search for remote jobs. The company is run by a remote team, true to its name and offers all kind of telecommuting jobs for stay-at-home parents. It also offers articles, tips and advice that will help land your job quickly.

Working Nomads (http://workingnomads.co/) – previously named goRemotely, this is an excellent list of remote jobs that will land in your inbox daily or weekly as per your preference.

Technical Job Boards

AngelList (https://angel.co/) – this is one of the best sites for startup jobs. To look for remote jobs, choose the "Remote OK" tab in the "job type" menu.

Authentic Jobs (http://www.authenticjobs.com/) – this is job board especially for web professionals. Exceptionally well designed and manned, this is a good starting point for developers and creative web professionals.

Dribble (https://dribbble.com/jobs) – this a site meant for web designers and web professionals. Well organized and easy to use, this is a place you can easily find a great job.

PowerToFly (http://powertofly.com/) – this site is relatively new, but it is dedicated to WOMEN tech professionals. It matches your profile to the jobs posted. This is a site started by two stay-at-home moms – dedicated to all stay-at-home moms out there.

Ruby Now (http://jobs.rubynow.com/) – this job site is dedicated to Ruby Developers hence, the name. You need to watch a video with instructions on how to get hired. You can then find access to some excellent opportunities in this field.

Stack Overflow (http://careers.stackoverflow.com/) – this is a job board that lists about 2,000 remote tech jobs.

Freelance And Contract

Fiverr (https://www.fiverr.com/) – this is a job board that lists micro tasks for just $5. It's a wonderful place to start earning doing odd jobs such as writing an article, designing an ad, photoshopping, etc.

Freelancer.com (https://www.freelancer.com/) – with over 13 million users, this site claims it is the largest outsourcing market in the world. You will need to bid for a job, which takes a little effort and time, but with so many jobs posted, you have a good chance to land a job quick enough.

FreelancerMap (http://www.freelancermap.com/) – this is a site listing remote IT projects for all levels of expertise.

Guru (http://www.guru.com/) – this is freelance site where you can get all type of jobs from writing to designing to developers. It has searchable database and it also send you job matches to your inbox.

SkillBridge (http://www.skillbridge.co/) – this job site is designed to tie-up top-notch consultants for short-term engagements. It could be marketing email campaign, or building a business plan – this site gives you the scope to become a well-paid consultant.

UpWork (eLance and oDesk merged) https://www.upwork.com/ – recently eLance merged with oDesk to create UpWork. This is a site where you can bid for any type of work such as writing, VA, tech, designer, etc. It also matches your skills and send you recommendations of jobs in your inbox.

General Job Boards

Career Builder (http://www.careerbuilder.com/) – this site lists about 9,000 jobs including part-time and remote with leaders of the industry. To search the database, type *"remote"* or *"telecommute"* in the search box.

Idealist (http://www.idealist.org/) – this a site that provides remote development-based work. Those who wanted to work in development field for Africa or India this is your platform. Select *"remote"* when searching for jobs.

Indeed (http://www.indeed.com/) – this is a tried-and-tested job board with more than 2,000 remote jobs listed. This is a great place to start your search.

Monster (http://www.monster.com/) – one of the best known job board in the world, you will find here a huge array of remote jobs that will fit any profile.

The Muse (https://www.themuse.com/jobs) – this site makes job searching fun with a easy-to-use and fun interface. It also provides you with up-to-date advice and information about the best available jobs.

Direct Selling

Avon (beauty) https://www.avon.com/ - an excellent company for "micro-entrepreneurship", where you choose your hours and work for satisfaction as well as profit.

Chloe & Isabel (https://www.chloeandisabel.com/) – similar to Stella & Dot this is a site which will help you set your own business at the level you feel comfortable. You can grow at your own pace while you make profit.

Mary Kay (skincare) http://www.marykay.com/- this is another company that provides opportunity to stay-at-home moms to start a business on their own terms.

Stella & Dot (Jewelry) http://www.stelladot.com/- this is a company started by a stay-at-home mom which is now big enough to offer franchise and direct selling work.

Trend Tribe (http://trend-tribe.com/) – this is a jewelry site that provides direct selling and remote jobs besides franchise model business opportunity.

CONCLUSION

This book is by no means an all-inclusive information capsule. This is rather meant to show you, the stay-at-home mom (and dad) that it is very much possible to earn as much if not more with a remote job as you would with a regular 9 to 5 job. In addition, you get to stay at home and look after your children ensuring that they are brought up with the love and care they so much deserve. This is a winner from all the angles possible.

It's no wonder that more and more parents – not all single – choose to start a home business or engage a remote job so they can enjoy more time with their family. I hope you find the book useful and you land a job that suits your talents and financial requirements.

Here is wishing you a healthy, happy and prosperous life!

Cheers!

WANT MORE ?

Phew! You made it and you are now on your way to becoming a millionaire mom!

I'm very grateful that you took the time to read this, so I want to hook you up with my future books.

If you want FREE downloads off ALL my future books, make sure you follow my Facebook page:

www.facebook.com/touchofwisdomm

I normally give away my books for FREE on the first few days of release.

I really hoped you enjoyed this book, and could this a positive review !

- Christina Elroy

Founder of A Touch of Wisdom

USEFUL RESOURCES

Free eBooks

These are a few eBook, which will help you find your niche as a stay-at-home mom. You will find advice, tools, sites and resources that will get you there.

1. Online Jobs That Can Change Your Life Today - http://workathomeresourceguide.com/wp-content/uploads/2012/08/Online_Jobs_That_Can_Chan ge_Your_Life_Today.pdf

2. Find the Perfect Work at Home - http://workathomeresourceguide.com/wp-content/uploads/2012/08/Strategy_For_Finding_The_P erfect_Work_At_Home_Job.pdf

3. WAHM Masters - http://www.perfect-typing-jobs.com/support-files/wahm-masters.pdf

4. Freelance Writing Guidance - http://www.authorspublish.com/download-the-authors-publish-compendium-of-writing-prompts/ or http://www.authorspublish.com/wp-content/uploads/2015/07/the-authors-publish-compendium-of-writing-prompts.pdf

Sites

1. Work-at-Home Job Boards - http://www.dreamhomebasedwork.com/work-at-home-job-leads.html

2. RookieMoms - http://www.rookiemoms.com/

3. Site that presents 36 How-To-Do Guides on Work from home - http://livelikeyouarerich.com/how-to-make-money-as-a-stay-at-home-mom/

4. SingleMomsIncome - http://singlemomsincome.com/

5. BusinessAmongMoms - http://businessamongmoms.com/

6. MojoMums - http://mojomums.co.uk/work-from-home-options/

7. Franchise ideas for stay-at-home moms - http://www.franchisedirect.com/information/womenin franchising/homebasedfranchisingforstayathomemoms /34/314/

8. More Franchise ideas - http://www.evancarmichael.com/Franchises/1164/Top -10-Franchises-for-Work-at-Home-Moms.html

9. Business ideas - http://www.theworkathomewoman.com/99-work-at-home-ideas-women/

Articles

1. 10 Top Paying Remote Jobs - http://skillcrush.com/2014/09/11/10-top-paying-remote-jobs/

2. 5 Common Myths - http://skillcrush.com/2014/07/08/5-common-telecommuting-myths/

3. Work from home leads - https://www.pinterest.com/lashayhudson/1000%2B-legitimate-work-at-home-ideas-for-stay-at-ho/

4. Money Making Ideas for Stay-at-Home Moms and Dads - http://www.yourmoney.com/credit-cards-loans/ten-money-making-ideas-for-stayathome-mums-and-dads/

5. Entrepreneurship for Stay at home Moms - https://au.pfinance.yahoo.com/money-manager/loans/home-loans/article/-/13739082/mumtrepreneurs-savvy-and-successful-stay-at-home-mums/